TO SEE WHAT I HAVE SEEN

SEE WHAT I SEE

Robert Wexelblatt

POEMS

Copyright© 2022 Robert Wexelblatt
ISBN: 978-81-8253-952-5

First Edition: 2022
Rs. 200/-

Cyberwit.net
HIG 45 Kaushambi Kunj, Kalindipuram
Allahabad - 211011 (U.P.) India
http://www.cyberwit.net
Tel: +(91) 9415091004
E-mail: info@cyberwit.net

Printed at Thomson Press India Limited.

ACKNOWLEDGMENTS

"Daydream," "The Coyote of Myrtle Avenue," "Mrs. Podolski Watches the News," "Mrs. Podolski Returns from a Visit," "Oneirology," and "So Long as We Exist" first appeared in *Modern Literature*

"Advice to a Distraught Friend," "Between High and Low," "Bicycle Poem," "Commonplace Crusoes," "Flinching Time," "On the Road Near Chiangling the Poet Chen Hsi-wei Encounters a Young Musician, Summer, 597 A.D.," "Hsi-wei in The Gardens of Shun," "Incerta Navigatio," L'Amour Quantique," *"Les Sinfonies* de Michel Delalande," "Mrs. Oleander's Marriage," "Mrs. Podolski Tells Me What's in Store," "Helping Mrs. Podolski Put Away Her Groceries," "What Mrs. Podolski Fears," 'New Neighbor," "Nothing's So Precarious," "Prosthetic Gods," "Report to Maggie," and "Under the Pavement, the Beach," first appeared in *Verse-Virtual*

"Bolting" first appeared in *Sou'wester*

"Birthday Epigram" first appeared in *Poetry Pacific*

"A Comedian," "Fran and Reg's Divorce," "Musing at the Outdoor Early Music Festival,"

"One Consolation," and "Patet Atri Janua Ditis" first appeared in *BlazeVox*

"Concerto" first appeared in *Carcinogenic Poetry*

"Cruel Month" first appeared in *Spoon River Poetry Review*

"Divine Wind" first appeared in *Crab Creek Review*

"Elelín," and "Fifth Date" first appeared in *Yes, Poetry*

"The Escape" first appeared in *Sou'wester*

"Every Now and Then I Think of William Penn" and "How About You?" first appeared in *Blast Furnace*

"Evolving Sonnet" and "To Have Seen What I Have Seen, See What I See" first appeared in *Orphic Lute*

"Fairy Tales" first appeared in *Eunoia Review*

"Five Little Nocturnes" first appeared in *Line Zero*

"Fourth Nor'easter of March" and "Nocturnes" first appeared in *Autumn Sky Poetry*

"Mrs. Podolski's Critique of Judgment" and "Mrs. Podolski on Pregnant Friends" first appeared in *Innisfree Poetry Journal*

"Good of You to Ask" first appeared in *Temenos*

"Hair Haiku" first appeared in *The Cape Rock*

"In Praise of Noah" first appeared in *Licking River Review*

"Juno Februata" and "Sex Is Too Expensive" first appeared in *Poem*

"Lorn Leopard" first appeared in *Write From Wrong*

"Mahler" first appeared in *Piedmont Literary Review*

"Me and Mary S." first appeared in *Southern Humanities Review*

"Mrs. Oleander at Windermere House" first appeared in *Grey Sparrow Journal*

"Slaughter, from a Distance" and "Six Mental Exercises" first appeared in *Orion Headless*

"The City" and "The Lion and the Honeycomb" first appeared in *Café Review*

"What Did You Learn Today?" first appeared in *Apt*

"You Might Just Think of Me" first appeared in *South Dakota Review*

Contents

Daydream

If I could play the piano and speak Italian
I don't think I'd do anything else, not
if I had Bill Evans' hands and Mastroianni's voice.

If I could play the piano and speak Italian
I'd be murderously cool, set the fashion
in clothes and jazz. I'd always be in, never out.

If I could play the piano and speak Italian
I'd be desired by women, envied by men.
I'd play "Quiet Now" and sigh *Sono un po 'triste.*

If I could play the piano and speak Italian
I'd have a blissful night-life, steeped in art—
two sets at Birdland, jamming at the Blue Note.

I wouldn't play just jazz but Busoni and
Scarlatti too, names I'd pronounce elegantly
if I could play the piano and speak Italian.

If I could play the piano and speak Italian
I'd give charming interviews, stylishly
laced with Florentine proverbs and Roman jests.

If I could play the piano and speak Italian
I wouldn't be a celebrity; I'd be
adored by a few thousand *connoisseurs,*

aficionados e cognoscenti
who'd invoke my name with warm, knowing smiles,
if I could play the piano and speak Italian.

Ah, che bel sogno ad occhi aperti!
All my words would be music, my chords poems,
if I could only play the piano and speak Italian.

Advice to A Distraught Friend

In the late rounds, slumping back on the ropes,
the jabs fall faster; the upper-cuts are rough
and keep coming. There's cheering from the dopes
in the cheap seats. I thought you'd had enough.

But you stand and take them, blow on blow
to the gut, the ribs, your head—why is that?
The fists persist, how low will they go
before you, or the towel, hit the mat?

For every minute you endure the news
give over five to looking at a tree.
That's my prescription. I myself would choose
a beech. Or, if it's near, stare at the sea.

Advice

Let those in, but stay outside;
close the door, but not too wide.

Bestir yourself while you're at rest;
your worst is better than your best.

They've patched the road around the hole;
you're well-heeled now, save for your soul.

The car's all gassed, the sky's black blue;
the clock runs backwards, three to two.

One meal a day makes not a fast;
an unstruck match is made to last.

Leave rooms that cough, they seethe with germs;
fish you can catch are full of worms.

You'd have two legs if you could dance;
don't wear a skirt beneath your pants.

Endure the weather, bear the news;
regret the future, rent the pews.

Let them all in after you go;
if they say yes, then you say no.

Between High and Low

My mother used to set out a special
glass dish when there was company. It had
a gilded edge, compartments for olives
and carrot sticks, a third for celery.
The celery was stringy so it was the
salty olives and crunchy carrots
I pinched, special treats, grown-up ones. At the
cocktail hour, I still favor a snack
of olives and carrots. No matter if
the olives are green or black, with pits or
hollowed out, the carrots Bugs-Bunny big
or faux-baby small. As they say, it's all good.
They're a fine match, carrots and olives, like
a loving couple drawn from different worlds,
one down from trees, the other up from dirt.
And I, between noon and night, like any
human child marry earth's gifts in my mouth,
briefly happy in this muddled middle state.

A BICYCLE POEM

If calculated a moment after the Big Bang,
the probability of a two-wheeler would have
approached zero; yet, in that mélange
of exploding gases, the bicycle was no
less inevitable than the starfish, the
Punic Wars, or the pneumatic tire.

Few articles made of Democritean
atoms ever become Platonic ideas,
capping their evolution, any innovation
bound to be a case of *Schlimmbesserung*.
Perfection should leave us awestruck:
the Stradivarius violin, the Starley Rover.

A few lessons learned:
Right of Way = Avoirdupois.
Virtue's price is vulnerability.
Phallic road-nails long to penetrate
soft round tires—usually the back ones.
There's always a bike that's
lighter and someone faster.
You've got to toil for your thrill:
uphill takes longer than downhill.
Even if some jerk in an F-150 isn't positive
he owns the road, he's damn sure you don't.

Fraternité, sororité—
the little nod, the tiny wave.

Et liberté—you aren't obliged to
nod and not required to wave.

Earbuds pumping out Brahms' *Second Serenade*
or Soler's *Fandango* as you outstrip mosquitos
on a Sunday morning—a moving Mass, solitary
Sabbath—biking past the SUVs arrayed outside
St. Aiden's, communing with I-Pod, sky, and road,
the Camelbak preserving cold, sacramental water,
knees, hips, and muscles all in proper working order:
on the seventh day you pedaled and it was good.

One blustery day there came unexpected rapture,
unearthly silence-in-noise and stasis-in-motion.
Your pace fell into a sudden alignment of
speed and direction with the wind; for ten
seconds, you were at one with the Anemoi,
matching the gust still whipping branches,
bending high grasses, whirling leaves while in
your bubble all was still as Lake Weishan at dawn.

At first it seemed impossible to stay up.
What? Me? On two wobbly, listing wheels?
But then a grown-up shoved you down a hill
and terror flipped to exaltation; you wouldn't
get off until dinnertime, got up early the next day.
After years of biking, you're certain you can't fall.
You were wrong then and you're wrong now.

Birthday Epigram

Age is the illusion mirrors make real,
a fact your adolescent soul belies.
Reflections don't reveal all that you feel,
just someone worn and wizened and not wise.

Bolting

first thing after breakfast, between math and
gym, in the fifth hour of a moonless
night, while somebody was locked in the
bathroom, im richtigen Augenblick,
between littoral and piedmont, down the
cellarway, on a twelve-speed bike, during
the halftime show, while remarking
outsides are roomier than insides

> Her hair's fragrance is so sweet
> yet his liberty's so dear;
> tonight he'll kiss her feet—
> tomorrow he's not here.

deciding between snare or love, weighing
a species of duty against a cunning
trap, just after recess, according to
plan, despite a blizzard, between Act Two
and Act Three, dodging around the corner,
before even knowing what she was up to

thereafter there's much dull placidity
and olive inanity of backyard grass,
gatherings of English sparrows, Sunday
silences, private migraine moaning,
unshared doubts and teleologies,
a solitary and vacant domain.

pull that taffy, stretch that gum
until the gossamer thread
severs in stillness like a
couple who never should've wed.

before learning how full the world is of
doorknobs, between white sheets that made their
legs look tan, prior to becoming disillusioned
with commodious salles de bain, while
distinguishing phony from unfeigned,
decades-old clouds cast shadows over
static lawns and then blew off, bugged out.

Consolation is the pleasure of soothed pain.
They were sometimes one: a May night in the rain
when they got drunk and laughed like they'd gone insane;
when she crooked her finger saying, Do that again.
Consolation is the pleasure of soothed pain.

Into dusk or dark, between dawn and
forenoon, lassoed horse from
makeshift corral, embezzler from cubicle,
hog from sty, fledgling from nest into
a cheerless mist of possibility.

A Comedian

Imagine, he said, a horseradish layer cake.
It took some time to conjure that up, then
a little more to get the point, nearly.
We guessed he meant you can make something
sweet out of what's bitter, or that looks sweet,
that the best jokes are going to bite back.

We thought he was an alchemist who
could transmute leaden pain to something bright,
yellow. We forgot alchemy's a cheat.
Bitter battles against bitterness he
fought, always victorious. We never
once suspected that he could lose the war.

COMMONPLACE CRUSOES

Solitary and cut off from
citizenship's consolations
with nothing but a private drum
to beat beneath constellations
silent as fringed rocks smacked by waves,
he sits marooned like a mourner
in a churchyard choked with graves
though life teems on every corner.

In the bleak hour before dawn,
with morning coffee, through the day,
in his bed, everywhere alone,
on the sidewalk, down the subway—
your desert islands aren't so rare
as maps insist; they're everywhere.

CONCERTO

the hero clamors against the mob,
square peg defying round holes

discord out of one and many
concord from many and one

a child noisily rebels and
the adults play along

one rejoices to lead the dance and
others, with delight, duly cavort

help me, and they succor
fight me, and they strive

join me, and they blend
admire me, and they do

temples, mansions, bridges
are thrown up, bar by bar

showing off, out of stillness
a complicated cadenza, soaring

in the middle, pensive meditation,
the solitary borne solemnly aloft

the journey like a romance, a war,
a life, tick-tock, strife to diapason

fugato to cadence and resolution,
helter-skelter presto until

all are spent, unanimous in
silence; only then. . . applause.

The Coyote of Myrtle Avenue

I suspect he's a Democrat;
something about the way he lopes.
For sure he's an atheist. Godless.
Brazen. The McCarthys' puppy's
missing but we're infested
with rabbits. And what about
the skunks? No civic responsibility.
Pays no taxes. Deadbeat dad. Lolls
around all day in his den, comes
out at night like a playboy or
a pimp. And I'll bet he marks
his territory too, peeing on
Mrs. Beckwith's peonies and
Mr. Bloom's Egyptian irises as if
the whole world belongs to him.
I saw him at one a.m. last night
trotting right down the middle of
the street. Bastard didn't even break
stride. I swear he smirked at me
with the contempt of a fund manager.
Thanks for the easy pickings, sucker.

CRUEL MONTH

My father was dead yesterday said
the drenched man into a dripping microphone,
to a moist lens. No, he's not broadcasting
anguish, I thought, not the ironyless
pain of the refugee expiring in
refuge, that last last straw. His stubbled face
isn't a furrowed waste of weeds at all
but a fallow field made sunny by
a miracle, that this very day his
defunct father has come back to life;
he cries for joy, yearning to proclaim to
us the marvel that has come to pass right
there in all that shit and misery.
It's Spring. Osiris, Tammuz, Adonis,
Atys, Lazarus. It's Easter Sunday,
1999. Holy Dionysius
greets the green world. Two daffodils have
just bloomed by the wall, sunny flowers in
the yellow sun. A sprightly mockingbird
is stabbing his sharp beak in the birdbath,
tail pointing pertly up at forty-five
degrees. But the illusion, the sublime
ambiguity, lasts just half a heartbeat.

Divine Wind, or Final Solution in the Suburbs

My neighbor went out and bought one of those
traps fashioned to snare troublesome beetles.
It's really quite simple. A specially manufactured
bag hangs from a sort of thick plastic cross
the sunny surface of which, like the inside of the
bag beneath, is treated to make it slippery, even
for beetles. Fixed to the cross is a stiff
sachet redolent of refined attar and just
above the scrotal bag's stuck a perfect square
precisely the green of healthy rose leaves in July.
When the sun strikes the trap the scent's
particularly strong, Mr. Wizard lectures warmly,
and the beetles, well, how can they resist?
The way it works, you see, is the iridescent
buggers, clumsy fliers but insatiable eaters,
crash into the bright plastic cross and slip
neatly into that expansive cul-de-sac. He nods,
he smiles. Lots of company and no escape.

Elelín

Between putative parental mountains
of diamond and gold Trapananda
nestled down, swaddled in Patagonian
fog, a tender Sleeping Beauty inside
impenetrable briars.
                                        She is a
legend never lost, never to be found
until apocalyptic hurricanes
drive every sublunary mist away.
Rumors sent two and a half centuries
of expeditions seeking for her, greedy
men and credulous, having learned hope and
cruelty from their fanatic priests.
                                                    In the
end, enlightenment seeped down even to
the barren foothills of the Andes, the
world contracted to a filled-in map,
and Trapananda, el Ciudad de
los Césares, fog-bound Elelín
never knew the lust she aroused; oblivious,
she never was surprised or kissed or raped.

Every Now and Then I Think of William Penn

Just one more spore infesting the round blue
earth burrowing in its wet green forests
scrabbling up its windy tors breathing and
burning avaricious bursting anxiously
extruding colloids, leaving lint where worms
worm their ways dry up inland seas under
my tears whole glaciers melt filthier than
scrofula boils canker an exceedingly
complicated pathogen shedding skin
my generations all heaped up like leaves.
   Once I cried, *"Look, I did something new!"*
   Now I sigh, *"Look, I'm doing something old."*

In May the afternoons grow long
drenched by birds in amorous song.
On what the race of worms consumes
the garden gradually blooms:
mixing ecstasy with hurt
stems battle skyward, up from dirt.
Disconsolate yet satisfied,
accepting all I once denied,
deposing the better with the worse
through the effrontery of verse.

Though I have most of what I need
I don't approve the life I lead,
cannot defend the nights I waste
or supersede my fatal taste.

I don't go in for maudlin strains
or tête-à-têtes on crowded trains,
loathe trudging through the swarming mall
and don't much care for phones at all.
      I will bear any pain
        if you let me complain.

It's sentiment makes one write of the heart,
one's heart, an eager self-deception
that even honesty can't redeem
that truth will underwrite dignity
as the gardener props a tainted rose.

That straight-man, that disciple, begs to know,
"O Master! Master, what is the Buddha-nature?"
The old monk scorns the faultless azure sky,
discounts the whiteness of a matchless cloud:
"Look at that stick of dried shit over there."
      Surely satori's a smash in the mouth,
        concussing cognition, stripping one bare.

What are the besetting sins of this poor
spore? Only his self-hatred and self-love,
both sharing his cell, that movable cube.
He longs for *apatheia*, the virtue
of those waiting so patiently in line
their virtue is visible least of all
to themselves, neither urging on the ones
before nor pitying the ones behind.
Can such virtue ever be consoled?

He stood by a river, muscular, brown,
too thick to drink, too thin to plow,

dense as some stupid metaphor,
yet he stared at it anyhow.
Like everyone he thought *one way before,
the other after*, thought *there goes now.*
    Can perpetual solitude atone
    for the mortal sin of being alone?

Brown rivers, apathy, enamored doves,
defective emblems of some lives, some loves.
Words open and close on the hinge of thought
sealing in the found and out the sought;
squeezed in this bag of skin I glimpse a door
and clutch the knob and wonder what it's for.

Evolving Sonnet

Evolution made you, do you think
for a reason? Evolution made
you reason, which isn't the same as
a sitting woman is remarkable,
inquisitive knees, wondering elbow.
I wish I might avid as a prix fixe
chewing up filet as a chick will
worms, not dejected by photographs
nor worn down by drizzling dossiers.

Evolution made me too it's true
and sitting on this blue world was
I green and will I ripe with love
for copper beeches, traffic jams, us,
stuck in this chamber of imagery?

FIFTH DATE

She:
We may stroll sometimes together,
at others not; moments will come
when we're at one; but enmity
can erupt in an instant, just
because of our affinity.
Similitude breeds sympathy
but not identity of mind.

He:
I love you and I disagree.

Fairy Tales

Once upon a time a complicated
cascade of fearful perils, parted lovers,
crooked shenanigans, confused identities,
unjust imprisonment, a usurpation,
a drop down an oubliette, a grave wound,
misplaced treasure, storms, shipwreck, a pack of
ravening wolves, mean stepmothers, furtive cutthroats,
inveigling witches—and yet it all wound up
so much better than any of us would
have hoped.

       Afterwards, waking from this
rapturous nightmare, we stared at one
another, amazed that life could be so
fervently lived, likewise charmed that on
those who suffered most should be conferred
this unheard-of joy, to tell over pains
grown dear, the tribulations that made folk
worthy of a happiness that would last
ever after.

       The next time, knowing how
it was to end, we were still amused but
not self-forgetfully enthralled, not slow
to propound aesthetic assessments, far
less anxious about those lost siblings, the
lame prince, that woodman's daughter, the third son.

Five Little Nocturnes

1.

The problem keeping him awake
is like a scratch on vinyl
splitting much-loved harmonies
with crisp, irrevocable clicks.

2.

Between midnight and three he thinks
not one thought. The quiet house turns
into lead around him, hardens
at last into gray thoughtlessness.

3.

She moans, she turns. In the light from
the street he smoothes her blanket down
then worries that he has trespassed
upon an alien, exclusive dream.

4.

A barrage of blackness pelts the
window with night; millions of souls
assault in waves. He wards them off
behind the soft crenelles of his sheets.

5.

The moon glints on the windowsill.
Scarcely disturbing the silence
he dances through rooms on his toes,
his arms embracing empty air.

Flinching Time

1.

Out of quiet swirl storms. A moment
and a day darkens, a second and
a heart shuts tight. Each instant's
gravid with menace, trembling with
miracle, with kettles about to boil.

2.

We're fast in time until time blurs
into weather, light, hunger, mood, sleep.
A reader in his chair is out of time;
a bather in her bath is timeless too.
Annihilation's just the fullness of time.

3.

For a spell there were no distinctions, no
news, then a happening happened in
a flicker we just missed, a gray shadow
passing over a brown wall. Occasions
occur in the catches between breaths.

4.

Head, trunk, knees, hands, toes, all torn apart.
Dionysus, shredded by a half-dozen
brutal titans gripping, dripping mud,
sinks from frenzied time to frozen silence—
perhaps to be reborn in sweet sane Spring.

The Fourth Nor'easter of March

Indignant neighbors all complain
that snow's still falling and not rain
or sunshine flecking pale green hills
with pools of yellow daffodils.
They whine that winter won't let go.
Weighed down with wet, belated snow
snapped branches mar the noiseless night.
Though dawn serves up a dazzling light
all value springs from scarcity;
snow's pretty when a rarity.
No matter if the statue's Greek
or if the storm's a thrilling freak,
they've wearied of the ceaseless sight
of beauty that's become antique.

FRAN AND REG'S DIVORCE

First intrigued next bewitched,
then enthralled, now unhitched.
Blame this sad conclusion
On the newlyweds' delusion:
What? Stay the same? Reg wouldn't.
Fran change? Oh no! She couldn't.

Fugue

Hearing it you forget to attend to
yourself just as on a roller-coaster
you never think about real estate,
groceries, loneliness. Dynamos, the
sawn cellos induce a charge, energy
fitting you for barricades and deathless
declarations, swollen by each voice in
rich consolidated chaos you're too
dumb and implicated to parse, mixed up
melody horizontal as Nebraska,
harmony vertical as Grand Canyon,
you feel like you're hugging an elephant
galloping toward a river in which to
leap will mean to be lustrated by mud,
all your stern, weak, importunate voices,
every petty dread and dream wedded once
and for all in resolute dissolution.

The Futile Lustration of Dust

Scrutinized the pencil space behind the toilet
after she left, fingered the Caucasian's fringe
and sniffed the panes, found everywhere hid
her hair, scent radiating from carpets,
drapes—all redolent. Even on the vacant
air weightless motes of her floated in yellow
sun below a ceiling groined by memory.

       Batter the blinds, flush the files,
        restore the rugs, twist the tiles,
       brush the basins, dust the doors,
       club the curtains, flog the floors,
       hose the halls, swab the ceiling,
       wash down walls, purge all feeling.

Raised an inquisition of rooms, racked,
screwed, exorcised, absolved one by one
the walls. *The heresies we should fear are*
those that can be confused with orthodoxy.
Still, sweeping it slowly into the pan,
weighing before sacrificing it down
the chute, still I blessed the harmless dust.

Good of You to Ask

Courtesy is being polite
when you don't need to be, when there's
slight consequence this way or that
as when the duchess asks the
gardener if his wife still suffers
from those frightful migraines.
Courtesy needn't mount as high
as caring, being to concern
as advice is to empathy,
as bad vermouth to good gin.
But you would like to know how I'm
doing, how things stand with me.
You are too polite, too courteous.

I'm point one percent lighter,
three-quarters of a percent older,
zero percent wiser, maybe less.
The spring, which takes up less than
sixteen percent of the year, has
kicked in on time and yet seems
twelve percent more ephemeral,
twenty percent less aromatic
than when I was, say, ninety percent
younger. I reckon my life to
be at least eighty percent over,
perhaps a bit more, probably
not less given the percentage
of cholesterol in my diet
and the dizzy percent of my

solitary hours spent with a pipe
in my mouth. I still drive at one
hundred percent of the speed limit
and a substantial percentage
of my CDs are of Bach's music.
I sleep about thirty percent
of the time, chiefly in the dark
after reading a negligible
percent of my current bed book.
I think my pension dropped about
ten percent last year.
                        What else?
I'm maybe two percent more lonely.
Hard to tell, but thanks for asking.

Hair Haiku

Any darker and
I would not have seen the one
hair on my pillow.

Dusk dropped. I picked the
brown hair from the blue linen.
Quickly, the sun set.

Graceful as the stroke
of Po Chü-i's brush, your hair
curled against my palm.

Absence and presence,
two mysteries clasped tight in
one hand. Empty rooms.

How About You?

After the chaplain finally shut off
the dripping faucet of his oily words

in which sense he felt was nearly made; after
his sister read his allegedly favorite

poem, three of his musician cronies
tramped up to the drums piano bass

secreted behind the pulpit and
rendered a loose and lachrymariffic

Someone To Watch Over Me, riffing with
eyes half closed though, given he'd hanged himself

in his office, no one there supposed he
believed anybody watched over him;

in fact, the Gershwin was a request from
his wife over whom he'd lovingly watched,

a truth featured in several eulogies,
who looked as though she'd endured successive

catharses after watching all the lost
plays of Sophocles and Euripides,

so drained of pity terror blood that she
scarcely noticed her two daughters, over

whom he'd also lovingly watched, one to
either side of her, fiddling with her skirt

staring across her at one another,
their perpetual war suspended by

this rude truce. He'd also watched, it seemed,
over colleagues, not all of them younger,

and students who looked at the wife as they
jokelessly spoke; the jazzmen played well

but we listened the way you do when the
music isn't meant for you. After the

song a minute of disquieting quiet
before the provost stepped up to declare

official sorrow, the sadness of the
secretaries vice presidents trustees

then suavely announced the scholarship fund
and where our contributions should be sent.

Maddening morning traffic we made the
slow-motion drive to the cemetery

whose ashes maples sycamores copper
beeches looked as if they'd live forever.

On the Road near Chiangling the Poet Chen Hsi-wei Encounters a Young Musician, Summer, 597 A.D.

Tallow leaves hang low, grass is brittle underfoot.
Birds spiral lazily then flutter down in the shade.
Prickly lettuce and withered jasmine
lie flat, like bing cakes baking on the dirt.
Paving tiles burn right through straw sandals.

Her eyes are so alert, it's as if she just found them.
The heat barely touches her, this devotee of song.
She's not the sort to compromise, not yet.
She asks me about music, what I've heard and whom.
Did I hear the great Zhang Chu in the capital?

Her reverence for her art exalts them both. She's
sure a celestial melody floats just above her head;
if only she could tug it down and play it then
the world would certainly change for the good.
The sun wouldn't scorch, perhaps taxes would drop.

She is small, delicate, nearly a child, though
if you look closely, you'll see that's half true,
that she's a soft soul in a hard cocoon.
Her faith is as unspoiled as her smooth skin.
Who would dare to scoff? Not me.

She asks my name and when I give it
I'm startled. She bows low, calls me Master,
can hardly believe it, tells me how much she

loves my old poem about Lake Weishan.
Her face is fervent as a praying monk's.

Taking up her liuqin, she begins to sing
and it's like running water by a dusty road.
I feel my forgotten poem surfacing from
Lake Weishan itself transformed, summoned
by the sudden beauty of this butterfly.

Hsi-wei in the Gardens of Shun

I passed through Shun last year in the
month of blossoms when new leaves made
the katsura branches look like mist.
The Duke's chamberlain summoned me.
We took tea then meandered through
the palace's renowned gardens.
Lord Zhang Tsu, my host, spoke of
the Orchid Pavillion Gathering. He asked if
I had ever seen the calligraphy of Wang Xizhi.

Behind the peonies stood a small pagoda,
an elegant thing, feminine and blue.
There the noblewomen of Shun stood together
swaying silkenly, like willows, shy as foals.
I found it hard not to look at them.
With a smile, the Chamberlain remarked
that, as Shun's ladies spoke only in demure
whispers, one would have to draw quite
near to hear their slanderous gossip.

In Praise of Noah

Delighted to be hostages to fortune,
someone's darling, too young to die at any
age: be happy that you've triumphed at life's
game of musical chairs, got things just right.
I admire the insouciance with which
you brush your teeth (or dentures), the sigh with
which you slide (or crawl) between the sheets,
certain somebody never sleeps so well
as by your side. On losers you know how
to beam like the Duke and Duchess of Kent.
When you promenade together down the
corridors, the space you take up moves with
you. The air suits you both like Armani.

Yes, of course I know it's not all peaches
and beer and skittles and cream, that there come
moments you'd gladly be one not two,
when, like the Peripatetic, you'd prefer a
cool friendship, could go for that bit on the
side, dream about the room of your own,
may even envy the bachelor's ill-luck.

But, in the end, what's to compare
with being someone's top priority, eh?
right there above the kids and groceries,
the point that's missing in pointlessness?
I can see from your cheeks somebody loves
to cook for you, will sympathize with your
head cold, knows just where to rub (yes, there!),

will take your side at dinner parties, and
by the hearth, where no rain dares penetrate,
plan cruises peopled by pairs and pairs and pairs.

Incerta Navigatio

You say you pray that we might stay
shipmates forever, come what may.
It's hazardous to supplicate,
my dear, for some impending date.

Who knows, of all the ships at sea,
which one's for you and which for me?
You might steam East, I could sail West.
Tuesday you might think parting best.

We all drift over an abyss;
nothing's vouchsafed, not even this
stout ship christened *The Here and Now*;
it lacks a rudder, even a prow.

My dear, while we're still safe ashore
in this dry room, behind that door,
let's be agnostics and not pray
for an unsure night, a doubtful day.

JUNO FEBRUATA

Between smeared sandstone arches
giggles of reveling boys seep into
the bloodied dungeon courtyard where
Pater Valentinus, apprehended for
succoring martyrs, remanded to the
Prefect of Rome, is reminded of
his broken pledges to apostasize,
soundly clubbed then, for renouncing
renunciation, decapitated. This on
the fourteenth of February, *circa* 270.

Why Valentine's Day, then?
hearts in place of clubs, arrows
and not axes? Why universal
cries of *Amor Vincit Omnia*?

Moved by their heathen hormones,
deemed lewd by the Church-At-Last-
Triumphant, Roman boys once daubed
on walls the names of favored girls.
The festival of Juno Februata fell
on the fifteenth. The bishops, resolved
to blot out this risqué festivity, to beat
it by a day, slice off its curly head,
ordained a sexless commemoration
of the martyred Saint Valentinus.

Yet paganism persists; beneath
the martyr's blood a red heart crammed

with chocolates, pierced by a half-
fledged Cupid—no cherub he, with his
stiff quiver and simpering mouth.
Secular Hallmark descends from the
scribbling of little Gaius, lusty Marius,
precocious Cato forming in magic
capitals (with or without lewd intent)
the names of their chiton-wearing
charmers. Valentine's name and day
survive as an unwilling apostasy,
as martyrdom trumped by love.
The basilica belongs to Juno Februata
who smiles a day early but cocks an
eye to spy out what Jupiter is writing.

L'Amour Quantique

What we observe is not nature itself, but
nature exposed to our method of questioning.
                    - Werner Heisenberg

And what if it turns out we are,
like light, waves one moment,
particles the next, not
intimate incarnate facts
but clouds of probabilities?

And what if, like electrons, we
can only claim a fixed abode
when rummaging around for it?

And what if that elusive but
vital article we call the self is
a species of whirling fictions,
a petite nebula and no mini-star?

And what if your brown eyes, fragrant
hair, thrilling voice, just-so nose,
your serious yet kindly mind and
that holy hollow behind your knee,
are no more than a cherished
yarn I tell my spinning self?

What if the you I love is nothing
like the you you are to you?

Les Sinfonies of Michel Delalande

There's more fun in his music than you'd expect
what with all the piping, tambourine-
waggling, castanet-snapping, goose-honking
and dog-barking. It's all a celebration,
punctuated sometimes by sobriety,
seasoned with a nearly tender sensuality.
But, really, it's meant for dancing. Even
the most bombastic passages, the ones
with kettle drums and horns, call up a
choreographed procession with studied steps.

Le Roi Soleil's court painters killed dead
in oils yards of tableaux-vivants
where the court is classically dressed in togas,
chitons, buskins, ersatz would-be ancients.
These are fun too, or funny, the privileged
faces simpering and unmistakably
French, the whole masquerade undermined by
Le Roi, tous les ducs, duchesses, les comtes,
comtesses, et même les petites enfants
sporting long, de-lousable wigs.

Is it a rule that the decadence of
the past should always seem nobler than that
of the present, that Versailles feels worthier
than Versace? Maybe it's true that the
patina of time redeems. Should the art
of the imperially privileged be
good enough—whether Greek, Roman, or French—

perhaps the depravity dissolves,
the foppery fades, and even the most
bloated pompousness may be pared down to
a sort of dignity.
          These days, Michel
Delalande, democratized, streams for cheap.

LORN LEOPARD

Dirt's dents dig rugged ruts,
and gravel's no gladsome guide:
between busted-up boards
all's deranged, detached, denied.

How do I fare? what
recklessly remember?
I might tell you on Monday
or maybe next November.

All Arkansas aches;
Maine's no longer cold;
dry and dour the Dakotas
and oh, New Hampshire's old.

Harmless, homeless, hopeless,
extant yet in exile
from your human face that
smiled, once in a while.

From me to me to me
from you to you to you—
unwired, wistful, watchful,
like a lorn leopard in the zoo.

Mahler

The music of death goes slow, is
deep; low moaning cellos beneath
a sinking sun, red like a scab,
hold up the occasional horn
fitfully marking fond farewells
to impatient scorn.

Saying adieux that last too long
risk the stench of sentiment,
casting Herakles for Hamlet,
scared by your long mournful bars,
we hasten to speed the silence
with our quick guitars.

Me and Mary S.

I dreamt I was Mary Godwin, enceinte, gravid with monsters,
a monster myself, likewise goody-goody Liz Lavenza,
inadvertent slayer of mothers, and also Victor
torn between an eight-foot doppelgänger and an ego-ideal
from Dullesville-on-the-Lake. Byron's briefly diverted;
Percy yearns to euphuize my prose, Polidari to get laid
like darling slutty Clare. It was on the Mer-de-Glace, that
other, anti-social lake, gelid as the pole, where I conceived
the catastrophic psychomachia of that wedding night;
my defunct children, begot on top of graves, my half-
sister dead by her own hand and my predecessor drowned.
Daily my father sent me back to the scene of the crime
where mother, breeder of a monster, lingered for ten
days, imagining her liberated daughter laden with rights,
but taught me instead this simple lesson: sex is death.

MRS. OLEANDER ON PREGNANT FRIENDS

Imparting the huge news in superstitious whispers,
smiling, serenely self-satisfied yet somehow sad,
anxious fingers feeling for quickening wombs,
declaring themselves officially ecstatic to be enceinte,
anything but ambivalent, husbands tumid with conceit,
yet underneath the paeans a hushed note of defeat.

They swell, consuming space and food, their gravity
growing ever more gravid like planetary giants
freezing in orbit, devoted Ganymedes waiting on
their hankerings, mammoth goddesses of nonce-cults
processing stately through trimesters like fraught
argosies, doing everything the books say they ought.

Some sail into harbor, plus-size panoplies with
topgallants unfurled, sure of admiration, vaunting
and mansion-stolid, immune to all mischance;
others, like cats, seem driven to secrete themselves
until the deed's done, turned inward as if seeing
a pristine way to love a pristine being.

Indulgence, sympathy, supportively mewing
over vanished ankles and multiplying chins,
never asking about the deep, the endodermic fear:
my duties are both contradictory and clear:
to admire without resentment, envy without disgust,
feigning sorority while they bear what they must.

Mrs. Oleander's Marriage

Lounging on her Robertson sectional,
she re-ran the lunch a frantic Missy
had begged her for, promising big bad news.
Turned out Doug was leaving Missy for a
temporarily pretty cliché. Missy'd
blubbered all over her Caesar salad
which exasperated Mrs. O., but then
even a happy Missy could do that.
Lunch unsettled her—it was Missy's fault.
Was the roiling near her navel anxiety
or gas? A pang turned her head; a cushion
slid softly to the floor. She straightened up
and surveyed her living room, shadowy
in the autumn light, a thing she hadn't
done for a decade. The room was reliable,
easy to ignore, stable and tasteful.

The coffee table looks keen to bark my shin;
the fireplace, dead from desuetude.
The paintings I've long ago lost interest in—
my Cornish landscape, his unsexy nude—
white carpet thirsty for a Bloody Mary,
the Chinese lamp sad not to be a vase,
the club chairs decorously stationary,
antiques indifferent to houseguests' praise.
The drapes hang like mutineers, defeated,
sick to death of being beige and pleated.

She gave a little shiver. Her home felt
so empty and hostile. Missy's sobbing was
so maddening that her sympathetic
platitudes all rang false as knock-offs. Missy.
Who could sympathize with a woman calling
herself Missy?
             But what of Mr. O.? Would
he displace her for one of his young
things? No need—they'd made their arrangements.
But if he tried, she'd hire that woman,
the one he said picked the bones of his fat
friend Phil, the lawyer all the men at the
club feared and nicknamed the Barracuda.
Fierce, toothy predators, barracudas.
She'd looked up pictures, noted the dead black
eyes, yoga-instructor bodies, the fins
like razors behind the lethal mouths. She clutched
her shoulders, shuddered. To brighten her
mood, she listed all the things she loved.

My amethyst necklace, going shopping,
dinners at La Maison Provençale, table-hopping
at the Club, Cecilia's organza wedding gown,
Mr. O. heading to bed early—or, better, out of town.
I've had my fill of men and likewise ladies
like Missy. But I do love my white Mercedes.

The nameless thing in her gut twisted, rolled.
For a moment the couch seemed to pitch and
the walls looked to be waving like lava.

What if one of his bimbos pulls a Boleyn,
claims sex before the wedding's a mortal sin?

I wouldn't much care if I were banished,
if this soulless house went poof and vanished.

She'd move from Winter to Florida, though
Palm Beach must be rife with Missys,
fragile cast-offs joining hardened widows
for the early-bird special while, just yards
away, the ocean teemed with barracudas.

The house would be sold. It's worth a lot.
I'll be all right for money, divorced or not.
And I'd get it all, more than half at least.
Your barracuda's an insatiable beast.

Mrs. Oleander at Windermere House

She needs assistance to live now. She's no
longer a she. She sometimes wonders who
she is, what she's saying when she gibbers.
Where is she then? She visits less often
than she should but more than she wants. Last time
she looked at her puzzled and scared. Nadège,
the Haitian nurse, merrily reported that
she still whips everybody at Scrabble.
She resented being told; felt it was a reproach.
She hates it here, the muffled hallways
freshened with a scent she calls Euthanasia
No. 5, the pathetic garden outside
the triple-glazed windows, that weedy
Japanese maple and sad arc of spirea.
Here there are only shes. She puts her hands
over her eyes. *To this favor she must come*
warns Hamlet, though Yorick wasn't a she.
She's less of a she herself. There were so
many men but now that's all over with.
She misplaced her libido last year or
the one before. La Change. She whines and knows
it's maddening but just can't help herself.
She'd gone through it too, so depressed she had
to take pills. She gripes to Mr. O.
until he finds some excuse to leave the room.
Her dentist frowned. She said her molar won't
bear another crown. She needs an implant.
An implant, that's what she called her conscience.
She endures blank days, whole weeks of bleakness.

She dropped the book club and tried binge-watching
but lost the threads. She gave up aquarelle
class and makes pointless trips to Bed and Bath.
She already has more than enough sheets, a
tower of towels, gadgets galore. She bought
a white-noise machine to get some fitful
sleep. Mr. O. did try for a while.
He talked her into a dinner party.
It left her in tears and she swore it was her
last. Cecilia seemed sympathetic but
she caught her hiding three yawns. Her friends play
bridge, do yoga, swim, read bestsellers. They're
power-walkers, globe-trotters, beloved
nonies and bubbies, adventurous cooks.
She envies the ones whose mothers are dead or
remarried. She wonders who she was, is
now. She wonders who is she. A wife with
a platinum Amex card and a white
Mercedes? The childless daughter her childless
mother can't quite place? Just the dissolving
referent of a peeled pronoun? She straightens
and steps into the room. She's sunk in the
big recliner, stiff as a doll. The TV
is advertising a tropical cruise.
She turns, looks anxiously at Nadège and
asks, speaking for them both, Who is she?

Musing at the Outdoor Early Music Festival

To be the Bach-begetting race
long after we and earth are dead
we shot his preludes into space—
bragging, as Lewis Thomas said.

Music is math plus mystery,
organized improvisation,
its source beyond both history
and Euterpe's inspiration
in misery, collaboration,
a hundred mouths, a single brain
too dead to hear an ovation,
brightness of trumpets, plash of rain.

Whatever we feel we can sing and by
that singing cause others to feel; our art's
a looping feedback of joy and despair,
stateliness and laughter, ample harvests in
soothed pain, rowdy glee, agreeable shocks
of scintillation. Shamed by so many
of our acts, we're always proud of our stories,
our joyful noises, the ways we crank up
the mute rainbows of our lives by dreaming
plots, harmonies, at once ephemeral
and permanent like extinct creatures sealed
in the amber of dark defunct forests.

Mrs. Podolski's Critique of Judgment

Certainty's the clothesline on which we pin
the wash of our unmentionable doubt;
the dubious laundry we take in to make
believe we're sure of what we're sure about.

Men love football and absolutes; they relish
games with the absurdest rules, disputes
furnishing their chief fun; what one gaily
asserts another merrily refutes

until they come convivially to blows
and end the evening bloody, arm-in-arm,
still wrangling over whether he was in
or out of bounds, fair or foul, right or wrong.

Men boast they need just the facts and the law
to transfix the truth and fill the jails,
to know who's responsible and what for—
but we women require more details.

Men guillotine the past and future, shoot
snapshots; for us events are not discrete
like eggs lined up or artillery shells
but spill into a story; life's not neat.

Was it to lunch or dinner he asked her
out? Was it for Friday or Saturday?
Did she aim to wound him by choosing that
dress, not phoning before she went away?

How did he feel about the man he shot
in the stomach, and did his mother love
him less than cigarettes, truck drivers, beer?
Did he mean it? What can laws and facts prove?

You shouldn't be too quick to judge, my dear,
especially when you're sure you've all the facts.
Bear in mind that cut flowers must be arranged
and how the bird's tale differs from the cat's.

Mrs. Podolski Watches the News

Yes, my dear, I saw about the latest
murder-suicide, a cop this time, a wife
who wanted out. Domestic violence—
it sounds like an oxymoron but
we can't domesticate rage, can we?
Did you catch the one about the eighty-
year-old ramming his Camry into Walgreens?
Thought the go pedal was the stop. The mind
slips like the foot. Memory muddles
its index cards; *le mot juste* eludes you;
names tickle the tip of your tongue. When the
marbles roll off the table, dear, people stop
praising the few you've still got. *Trop vieux pour*
les crimes passionnels, pas les accidents de voiture.
The Toyota and the service revolver.
Despairing seniors aren't photogenic and,
as a rule, their suicides are solitary, quiet,
and seldom make the obits, let alone the news.

You must have noticed, dear, how the news
isn't new, every night the same uninspired
sonnet sequence of fires and traffic jams;
every evening yesterday's four-act play.
First a medley of bad things that happened that day,
next a weather forecast that could be over
in two minutes but maunders on for ten,
then the bouncy sports report from some broad-
shouldered bloke, and, for a finale, something
cute about a kitten rescued from a sewer, say,

or an infant delivered by a dazed cabbie.
The Six O'Clock News is aimed at the old.
Just look at the ads between the Acts
for laxatives, hypertension, acid reflux,
breast cancer, depression, arthritis, fading
memory, annuities, reverse mortgages.

The old can lose perspective like Celia Vetus
who got addled and said the world's going to hell
because of some minor drug bust in Malden.
Mostly, though, seniors take the news in stride.
We've got more aches than stress because you grow
detached, a spectator way up in the cheap seats.
The worries about the grandchildren are sincere
but abstract—hell, the kids themselves get more
abstract every year. *Abstract*, dear? It means
to draw away from. They wax, we wane. Newborns
in their cribs don't know they've got a future
while the doting grandmothers know they don't,
at least the ones who can still do the math.
Four years ago feels like yesterday; four
years of news just whizzed by. Four more
and we'll be where news is never made.

Mrs. Podolski Returns from a Visit

Hardly any left, my dear. It's the way of
the world. Events come in waves, you'll see—
you already have. Remember all those
weddings you went to last year? Six, wasn't it?
Well, get ready for a tide of babies and
suburbs. Divorces next, second marriages,
cruises, la Change, retirement, Delray Beach,
assisted living, then assisted dying
and the final milestone in the boneyard.
They told me her cancer's insatiable,
gobbling up organs like peanuts, spreading
like that fire last summer in Washoe.

          The hospice people
are all saints, at least when they're on duty.
Her daughter burst into tears when she saw me
because of what I represent. I hugged her,
of course. The son was stoic. He just shot
me a says-it-all nod. Edith and I met
fifty years ago, giggled, gossiped, played gin.
Today I had to say goodbye.

                    It was
when I hit puberty that it hit me, dear—
that no matter what bandwagon I hopped
on, notwithstanding sororities and proms,
in spite of book clubs and mahjongg teas,
shopping runs and girls' nights out, despite
dinner parties and July Fourth jamborees,

I'd wind up alone—it struck me that
half of life is just pretending otherwise.
When the end gets near the delusion dissolves;
we see it was always rushing toward us
like a murderer with a kitchen knife
galloping across the city to our bed.
We see that what we thought was long is short.
I know, dear, these are old people's thoughts,
unseasonable in every season. No doubt
that's what the King said to himself when in
Jarrow Old Bede told him life was just a
sparrow streaking through the mead-hall,
in one window and out the other.

Edith may have been glad to see me,
just as I'm happy to see you, my dear.
She might have wanted to say goodbye too.
But she'd collapsed into herself so
   I don't really know.

Mrs. Podolski Tells Me What's In Store

The first sign is when you find yourself
grousing more about the next generation
than the last. Nothing new in that, my dear.
Today's youths are rotten from the bottom of
 their hearts. They are malicious and lazy.
They will never be as youth was before.
Some archaeologist—or, I like to think,
a grad student—dug up a pot in Babylon
and found that inscribed on it. I can just
picture that potter, pissed off with his
scoffing teenage brats and their feckless friends.

An alternative formula is $N + 5$,
favored by the ironic and the vain.
What's N? However old you happen to
be, my dear. When I hear some crone or geezer
lauded for being *young at heart*—never
mind a coronary may be minutes
away—I'm not sure if it's down to a
resilient spirit or mere childishness,
though I suspect plain hard-core denial.

You've time yet, dear. Anyway, it's hard to
be sure when somebody's middle-aged.
It was fifteen for Franz Schubert, nine for
poor Tom Chatterton. Of course, you could say
they never got so far. But some need no time
at all. Take Aristotle—the man was
middle-aged at birth. He's like the uncle

who's seldom wrong but often boring.
The *via media* isn't exactly
inspiring as ideals go, is it? I've
always felt Plato was the younger man.

Not to worry, my dear. Sufficient unto
the day. You've time yet with that porcelain
complexion and burnished hair. But middle
age will come and, for most, it's a plateau
stretching over decades, flat as Kansas,
until you're sure it's everlasting and
you drive on until threescore-and-ten
rears up like Mount Elbert, a peak so tall
and biblical even the faithless can't deny it.

Helping Mrs. Podolski Put Away Her Groceries

Yes, pork chops. I cut off the fat and wrap
them separately in plastic, my dear. Thanks.
I know I shouldn't eat them but they were
on special, and they were Mr. P's second
favorite dish—porkchops with baked beans and
applesauce—so they're for old times' sake. His
first favorite? Roast beef and potatoes
with green beans or cauliflower, all of
them cooked to death, the way his mother did
them. In time, he'd tolerate a little
crunch in his vegetables and a blush
in his beef. Over the years, I even got him to
spread out as far as the occasional
lasagna and stir fries over white rice.
He preferred beef to chicken or pork and
spit out my one attempt at tofu.
Well, in fairness, so did I. No take-out
but his precious pepperoni pizzas.
Would you wash off those potatoes, dear—and
just set them on the drainboard?

Talked to him once about becoming
a vegetarian. Fat chance. We've always
eaten animals, he claimed, speaking for the
species. It's in our nature, like razing
forests and dumping the waste overboard.
In his opinion, shitting upstream from the
camp's in our genes. Nietzsche thought so, too:

exploitation belongs to the essence
of what lives. . . But, my dear, all the cow farts
and ex-rainforests!

　　　　　　　　Saw this young scientist
on TV and thought he meant to flatter us.
A spectacularly successful species,
he said, then I caught the irony—it's like
calling the bombing of Hiroshima
a proficient job of urban renewal.
Well, we can't live without our steady fix
of diffusible molecules; stones won't
do and meat tastes good; but the more we eat the
worse things get for us and the world. When the
heat thuds down, we up the air-conditioning,
burn more ancient algae, a deadly cycle.
If to live is to exploit, then is the
only answer death? But who wants to hear
that salvation requires starvation?
　　He may live without love,
　　what is passion but pining?
　　But where is the man
　　who can live without dining?
That's Bulwer-Lytton in a genial mood
during the Industrial Revolution.
Yes, dear, the-dark-and-stormy-night guy.

Mr. P. didn't start out sclerotic but,
like his arteries, he got more so and
wound up believing our DNA is as
conservative as a Georgia Republican.
What do I know? Maybe it is. But the
genes can evolve, can't they? Opposable thumbs,
less hair, bigger brains?

Did you see it hit
a hundred-and-eighteen in Siberia
last week, dear? Siberia. Way things are headed,
nature's going to turn on this successful
species and she won't spare the vegans. Old
folks have much to answer for, unthinkingly
gunning our V-8s , heaping up the national
debt, outliving the Social Security
actuaries' projections—so selfish.

Nietzsche was too mad a prophet to be
consistent, too sensitive a seismograph.
He extolled the planet's beauty but knew
what spoiled its complexion. *The earth has a skin,
and that skin has diseases; one of its
diseases is called man.* What was that, dear?
Progressive but sexist? Maybe, but I
don't think he meant to let women off the
hook—or that he hated us. Read him closely.
I think you'll see he was afraid of us.

Oh, the cold cream and shampoo? Just set them
aside, dear. I'll take them upstairs later.

What Mrs. Podolski Fears

My dear, you must have noticed how my tongue
squirmed over the name of that actress and
the title of the novel I wanted
you to read. I know you've seen me frown and
rummage through the middle of a sentence.
It's as if the verbs are children playing
hide-and-seek, making faces and giggling
in a closet. Am I frightened? Not of
death but death-in-life, not of ceasing to
be but of being mentally flayed inch
by inch like poor Vivian Malatesta.
Did I tell you her daughters took her away
on Monday? Nothing else for it, I know.
To this favor and all that. They put her
in the same joint where I visited Gert
Rosenbaum last year. Gert, a whiz at bridge,
Gert who published on set theory. They call it
Windermere House, as if it hosted
fox hunts, country weekends. Spruces and spirea,
pleasant staff, decent food, inoffensive
paintings on cream-colored walls, board games,
heaps of old bestsellers, big-screen TVs.
Top-of-the-line. It's clean and tidy and
horrible. I fled.
                   About a year and
a half ago, Viv phoned me up and begged
me to rush over. She sounded desperate.
A fall, I figured, or bad news about the kids.

How about making us some tea and then
I'll read you my notes. Yes, I've been making
notes, and in rhyme, to exorcise and exercise.
The first is about that day it started with Viv.

Something went missing—a spoon or a book.
She couldn't say what or where we should look.
Was it her compact or a wedge of cheese?
Something was missing—the remote or her keys.
She rifled the Civic; I looked under the bed.
We didn't know then that it was her head.

It's like planing a board. One curly sliver,
another swipe, then more, until, at last,
the board's no more than a vestige of
itself, a ghostly wooden vacancy.
Am I afraid? I don't want to find out
what I'll be when I can't remember this
room, snatches of Yeats and Stevens, Evans
playing *Peace Piece*—or you, my dear—when
there'll be no self left for me to lose.

Yes, I know I'm not Viv Malatesta but
it doesn't cheer me up, though my mother
would think it should. *The secret*, she loved to
say, *is comparing down, not up*. I think
she said it less to instruct me than to
convince herself she was content with her lot.
One day, she pointed to this man outside
the Acme holding up a sign. It said
"Will Work For Food." See? *Compare down, not up.*
Well, her advice is sound enough but, when
the storm breaks, of little use. What Mother

knew was the secret of settling, not of life,
of capitulation, not happiness.
Others are worse off? Yes, I've a roof and an
income and haven't yet forgotten who you
are, my dear. My mind to me a kingdom
is, and it hasn't yet turned into Lear's.
All the same, I keep forgetting things, words
fly out of reach; every lost memory feels
like a caress from the feather of dementia.
You'd like to cheer me up, reassure me.
And so you do—at least you do the first.

Last night I slept badly. I dreamed about
Vivian and Mother, got up and scribbled this:

Think of a homeless woman and her cart
not the famous painter and her famous art.
Count your blessings, Mother smugly said,
stuck in a marriage that seemed to me stone dead.
Counting your blessed blessings comes up short;
it might be wisdom, but only of a sort.
What help to think of Beethoven gone deaf?
Cold comfort when you forget abcdef.
Poor Viv left pieces of her brain behind.
Beethoven lost his hearing, not his mind.

New Neighbors

The new neighbors' new baby was born a
month after they moved into their new home.
The wife is exceedingly pretty and
knows it, as does her husband. There's something
of the ballet about them—he's the stem,
she's the rose. They own an SUV and
a sport sedan, both German; even their
all-day baby-minder drives an Audi
Q5. Every third day, he mows the lawn and clears
the cuttings with a hundred-decibel blower.
She's seldom out-of-doors, not even to
take the baby for a stroll. He plays golf;
she entertains young women like herself—
sleek millennials with expensive hair.
On weekdays, the two drive off together
as soon as the Q5 pulls in. To work?
The gym? Their yacht? The sprinklers go off like eight
old faithfuls even when it rains. I took
them cherries on moving-in day and, when
the baby came, a toy. A thank-you note
showed up in my mailbox six months later.

Another young couple bought the house next
to theirs. They also have two cars and a baby
delivered soon after the moving van
drove off. I took over another toy.
The wife seemed annoyed that I rang their
bell just to offer a soft toy. This
time, there was no thank-you note at all.

I've never seen these four people exchange
a word or wave. They're self-contained, like
planets or pool balls. I wouldn't call
their predecessors gregarious, but
they waved, said hi, stopped by, chatted, asked
how it's going, gave me their medical
updates, offered and accepted help when
needed. To them, I was once the new neighbor.

Other people are a mystery. Even
with good looks, money, new houses and thriving
infants, couples can still be unhappy.

It's a comfort, somehow, knowing
they'll never wonder about me.

Nocturnes

Raindrops strike the island leaves like toddlers'
fingers on innumerable keys:
passion *piano*, fury *forte*. In her
bedroom his mistress uncrosses her legs,
lights up a cigar, and scribbles another
thirty pages on free love—to put down
her conscience perhaps, because, *comme les bourgeois*,
she believes productivity justifies all.
Chopin had small hands, but then the keys
were smaller too. When did pianos grow big
keys, and why? The way Rubinstein plays you
think this has got to be what Chopin heard
as he sat, coughing and calculating,
heard with full heart just before, with precise
pen, he set down these diaphanous dances
for Franco-Polish nymphs.
                              He wrote the first
in Mama's Warsaw, three years before he
moved to Papa's Paris to triumph as
a fragile lion of the salons,
irresistible with his *comme-il-faut*
name and *accent séduisant*. Twenty years
later came the last. A whole career of
moods realized for the rising breasts of
femmes romantiques, those for whom peignoirs
are pressed, erecting these iron armatures
festooned with feathers.
                              The beauty of illness
is rarified but persuasive. Is it
the fatality of his nightly sickness we
that makes health feel coarse and daylight crude?

Nothing's So Precarious

The given world conceals its fragility
in cattail meadows, beechwood forests, in oceans
too wide to poison and songbirds in clear air
with hidden hooks of plastic everywhere.
We think a solid scrim's behind our mortal motions
yet nothing's so precarious as stability.

We rely on and so deny the fragility
of the Constitution with its iron sides
and rights, the job on which home and food depend,
the eternal pyramids that nothing can upend,
City Hall and church, families, seasons, tides.
Yet, what's more precarious than stability?

The firmament underwrites our tranquility
though a slight shift of orbit or some novel germ
running like a vicious rumor through a school
or the reckoning from burning all that fuel
could bring a world pregnant with death to term.
There's nothing so precarious as stability.

One Consolation

As we grow older so the world grows
more complex, and more forgetful too,
as if wisdom and ignorance joined hands,
pressed cheeks, and staggered through a clumsy dance
to time's swift jigs and slow sarabandes.
Life's banal days and undistinguished nights
must not be despised since they're all we can
return to from our odysseys, our flights
through exotic latitudes, from our dreams.
Though quotidian tunes weary our ears
with routine rhythms punctuating years,
such music's always sweeter than it seems.

Oneirology

A dream from this morning, a lecture dream.
For once, there were no jokes, no digressions
or asides, not even one for instance.
My topic was serious and I was
suitably solemn. I even had notes.
The lectern was walnut. The hall was full
and quiet, like a movie theater
without a movie. I spoke into silence.
My words were silent too; yet nobody
cried *Louder*, no one spoke *Speak up!* The crowd,
all male, sat still and stiff, serious as
the officers in Frans Hals' *Banquet*, but
without the ruffs and sashes. What was I
preaching about? Danish theology? Crimes
Against Humanity? The national debt?
Couldn't remember, still can't. What I do
recall is the statuesque white goddess
looming right behind me, staring over
my head, dour, unmoving and unmoved. The
lecture was nothing. The urgent questions that
woke me were: why a goddess and which one?
Not Artemis—no bow.
Not Aphrodite—way too severe.
Not Demeter—no sheaves.
Not Tyche—not capricious.
Not Hestia—the opposite of homey.
Maybe Hera—but why would *she* be there?
No, it had to be Athena. It was.
Or Minerva. Stern, likely disapproving.

Goddess at once of wisdom and of war.
Was I lacking one, stumbling toward the other?

Another lecture dream, a nightmare I
had twice, premiere then re-release, when I
was in my thirties. On the lectern lay
a stack of notes, single-spaced, minuscule
font, paper legal-sized, the sentences
Teutonic, turgid, interminable.
Both times, the subjects were Dostoyevsky,
Kierkegaard, Kafka—*Notes, Fear and Trembling,
Metamorphosis*—all three, seriatim
then jumbled up. My lecture was pedantic,
disorganized, delivered in a monotone.
I read for an hour before looking up.
Before me, rising in the amphitheater,
rows of students, unaccountably rapt.
I resumed reading for a second hour
before looking up again, astonished
to see the hall still full, the same young faces
still entranced. I shrugged then droned on for
a third hour, voice cracking, eyes aching
and squinting to make out the tiny print.
The third time I looked up, I saw faces
unchanged, still eager, looked closer and
saw they weren't real faces, not real students
but painted ones. Horrified, I turned toward
the door that should have been on the left, to flee.
But where the door had been I saw
a multitude of receding halls with
me at the podium. I wheeled to the
right but that door too was gone, replaced by
another infinity of halls with

me before the terrifying *trompe l'oeil*.
I woke in an August sweat, trapped between
a brace of mirrors, past and future.

There are dreams that outstrip reality,
dreams that mystify, rising almost to
the surface then plummeting, dreams that tease
and smirk and slip beneath the door, into
the walls; amorous dreams that torment with
yearning, concupiscent or sentimental.
Dreams can inspire, pose or and solve conundrums
as the busy brain turns on this, off that.
Pharaoh's seven cows.
Paul McCartney's *Yesterday*.
Mendeleev's Table.
Mary Shelley's Monster.
Elias Howe's cannibals.

One afternoon, decades back, dog-tired,
I fell on my rented cot, instantly
asleep and instantly dreaming. I
sank through blanket, sheets, mattress, down into
a darkness that embraced me like some tender
fate or welcome death. I was barely twenty-one.
My basement room was thick with books and stale
Lucky Strike smoke. Lightless depth, meaning what?

Nightmares terrify, chastise, prophesy.
In the cortex, the censor dozes off,
neglected guardrails drop, memory and
fantasy turn feral, then there's the bottomless
abyss, the censorious Athena,
the baffling mirrors, seeming to unearth

buried truths, but all just out of reach.
For its health, the mind requires that we dream,
the doctors say, demands us to forge in
its fires metaphors and motions
that could signify nothing and yet
might mean anything, everything.

Patet Atri Janua Ditis

Now's she's gone and got cancer. Cancer.

Through these years apart, and all the ones
before, I liked to imagine her coming
to visit me in my final illness,
warily opening the steel door, her
breath just catching at the sight of my
state, taking reluctant steps across the
linoleum, how the starched hospital
sheets would sigh beneath her as she sat
tentatively, sideways, the way people
do, four fingers stroking my mottled
hand to console me, her still, silent face
saying everything I'd ever longed to hear.

I thought that would be terrible enough.

Prosthetic Gods

We have computers, smart phones, Zoom;
a flat screen in the living room
that's full of fluffy comedies
and earnest documentaries;
our cars direct us where to go,
say which route's quick and which one's slow;
a cube delivers corny jokes,
French recipes, the signs of strokes,
and plays us reggae, acid rock,
Miles Davis, and J. S. Bach;
we've indoor bikes made in Guangzhou,
a gizmo for strong espresso
that wakes us up, goes down like silk,
and even lactates frothy milk.
The big, the small, the far, the near
are visible; we've built the gear
to see the birth of a new star
and forests deep in Myanmar.

Yet when we're without screen or phone
at 3 a.m. and all alone
they're back, all the old dreads and fears
with just the music of the spheres.

REPORT TO MAGGIE

Dear Maggie, here's the résumé:
Today was just like yesterday.
Ate my breakfast at breakfast time;
Tried to compose something sublime,
Failed; washed and dried my shorts and socks
Then played an English suite of Bach's.
For dinner, pasta with that sauce
You like. Still, not a total loss
Because I got in a bike ride.
Round midnight, I tried to decide
Whether to commit suicide.
Obviously, I chose not to
(Though perhaps I really ought to).
Tomorrow, I'll labor and pray—
Bet it'll be just like today.

Sex is Too Expensive

Cecilia ran up fearful debts,
Gertie's games were unerotic,
Jane's husband made specific threats,
Emily turned out psychotic.

When Sue took me to meet her folks
They insulted and abused me.
Christina never got my jokes.
As for Betty, she just used me.

With Pamela I truly tried.
She shot me down by telephone:
"I said I loved you? Well, I lied!"
Go argue with a dial tone.

Long weekends wear away the soul
And New Year's Eve distills distress;
Summer levies a hefty toll
In vacancy and emptiness.

Yet one can stand a pain that's dull;
You only pay a monthly rate.
To sink funds in a life more full
Makes shy investors hesitate.

A couple walking hand in hand,
Her smooth content, his rugged pride,
Pairs and pairs stretched on the sand—
Envy costs less than suicide.

Julie's breast held a fist of bone;
I gave her up and nearly died.
Now, excise paid, I sleep alone.
Eros, I trust you're satisfied.

Solitude's an expensive art
Beyond the means of fools who weep
And to their sleeves affix their heart.
Still, resignation isn't cheap.

Slaughter, from a Distance

Majolica plate with stone-ground crackers
laid out like coins around a block of cheese
that tasted faintly of foreign goats; black,
green, and maroon olives in one crystal
bowl, another for the pits, one more for
salted cashews. Outside the children squealed,
romped on a trampoline screened-in for
safety. Our team was coming from behind
and we leaned closer, provisionally
enthralled. Suspense, tentative cheers, groans at
a penalty, breaths held until the arcing pass
was caught and three o'clock sunlight poured through
linen drapes like a blessing. And when our
men tied the score we rose like sportive gods
gazing down from their mountain. The machine
guns, mortar shells, the billowing acrid
smoke, screams and dismembered smears of red all
lay far beneath the sylvan horizon.

Six Mental Exercises

One
Think of moving as a way of standing still.
Two
Think of standing still as a way of moving.

Note how the first exercise
causes you to concentrate on
yourself; the second on the world

…and when you think of yourself
moving as a mode of not moving
you will hear the world panting to
catch up with you while, at the same time,
you are racing to keep up with the world

which, when you are performing
the second exercise, becomes as
still as you are, and, not
batting an eye, stares at you like the dog
who has given up chasing his tail
and now awaits his necessary walk.

THREE
Pretend you are an ancient Chinese poet in ancient China.
Four
Pretend you are an ancient Chinese poet when and
where you are living now.

Note how the first exercise
causes you to become sensitive

to brooks and trees, one might
even say to love them; the second
to be jarred, displaced, forlorn

…when you pretend the first
the world and your garden become one;
the transfiguration of the smallest cloud
is more telling than a change of emperors

who, when all of them are gone,
their dynasties preserved only in
a few perfect porcelains, a flourish
of calligraphy, a map-like landscape,
may seem not to have been such philistines

Five
Imagine everyone has died but you.
Six
Imagine you have died while everyone else still lives.

Note how the first exercise makes
life seem oppressive, like a curse,
while the second bids it so dear
that you can think of nothing else

…and when you imagine yourself
alone—alive alone—what do you see
but gray ragged cities over which
the wind draws itself up like a shroud

which, in the second exercise, is over
you, and that's how children picture
ghosts; so you too grow a ghost and
moan with envy every Hallowe'en.

So Long as We Exist, Death is Not with Us

You on a motorcycle, I in a balloon.
The road moved, and the clouds.
We moved. You fast and low,
I palely high and wanly slow.
My Uncle George ate a spoilt oyster.
Your grandfather went mad.
Two and a half wars broke out
like Cousin Zelda's acne, real bad.
You showed me me in a photograph;
it's a sort of proof, a negative,
you said, ocular proof, you said.
Somebody had a child or two
and one of them dropped dead.

But When Death Comes, Then We Do Not Exist

Silence isn't silent, sleep isn't sleeping,
darkness isn't dark, meaning isn't meaning.
The sandals on my feet I will not feel,
the blushes on the beach I will not feel.
History comes to many ends
by several means, you said:
that was your invariable lesson.
Shall we lie down now, shall we?
See? the bed is well made now.
Don't worry, you said, because the
coffee is already cold. But I'll miss
the breezes I'll miss, I said. I will.
Goodnight, you sighed, then gave me a kiss.

Under the Pavement, The Beach

Paris 1968

Certain we were the People, not a mob,
that the streets belonged to us, we surged,
the city's young blood bright red with zeal,
swarmed through the broad boulevards intent
on hammering each straight and rigid line
into the shape of a dancer's thigh or a
post-adolescent breast. How could the
bureaux and the banks resist a million
mouths raging for liberty and pleasure?
So we tore up everything that was tearable,
from toothpaste ads to frangible asphalt,
tossed it all skywards, glasswards,
policewards, parentwards, Godwards.
The old needed to be shoved aside and yield
us what we yearned for, endless August in utopia.

Sure, we were foolish, drunk and callow, but so alive.
We plastered the city with mottos of preposterous politics.
    Reins to the children, guns to the Seine.
    You have your money—we, our hair.
    Raise high the guillotine of love!
    Beneath your filthy pavement, the clean beach.
These we sang out, chanting each to each,
raising fists and voices, strong just from taking part.
Those silly sidewalk slogans can still touch the heart,
naïve poems, fiercely unresigned and unalloyed.
Is it just as well we failed, grew older, and employed?

The City

slugs it out with i-beams, jersey barriers; is raucous, full of heart;
draws up to her full supercumulus height, scrutinizes you indifferently,
then spits like a beer-swilling riveter. Inside coats and shoes the
nude commuters daven, furtively looking only inward, faces arrayed
like melons at the grocery, hands and navels identically unique,
their variegated soundtracks trembling under fixed phones,
Mahler and Metallica, Marley and Milhaud, Eminem,
Moussourgsky, Motown and Martinu—music endlessly wrought,
composing incessant prayers that seep up rusty brick walls,
ooze along formed concrete, around windows double-glazed against
unprayerful noise; spurts with energy congealed to money,
ambition thick as failure, empty and full; sings its elephantine
fugue where every modulation is plausible; is lava flowing
chunky with imaginable presents and every gift that's not;
is thunderous diapason of diapasons, blizzard of blizzards;
is infinite catalogue of catalogues, thing of things.

Samarkand and Machu Pichu, Nineveh and Troy, Sodom and
Las Vegas, all great cities have their age of gold and glory,
are eternally transient, evanescent as old reveries,
durable as granite and flimsy as reticulated webs.
God levels his great eye on cities to punish or exalt, to
ruin them as emblems, aims His huge finger at them as to say
*This is what I charge you to build, I want walls, libraries, bodegas,
ghettos, schoolyards, hot-dog stands, electric grids, trash trucks,
sewers, playgrounds; I want bullies and brokers, matrons and
call girls, lawyers and legal heirs. Go on, add, subtract, multiply, make a
city of yourselves spread out like the theory of bodies, like My
immense Leviathan, make a Behemoth of patiently accreted cells,*

just as I made you; let it drift through time and space, through dreams and history; make yourselves a mega-homunculus animated by greed and holiness, and I shall make it mortal, just like you.

The Lion and the Honeycomb

"How can you love yet mock me so?" A pout
on her moist lips, "That's what I'd like to know."
He puffed his chest with air then let it go
and pushed her toward the bed. "Well, if you doubt—"
She scratched and wrestled free. He laughed, "Such scenes
you Gentiles make! All right, I'll tell you
a fourth time. I'm a hairy Jew who
can slay or screw a thousand Philistines."

Is the strength resolved in sweetness holy?
She drew her sleek legs apart so slowly
he couldn't stop himself but thrust aside
the samite from her scented thighs. Killers
armed with scissors likewise spread them wide,
trusting pillow talk and gods on pillars.

What Did You Learn Today?

In History we're doing China. The book says
that Emperor Wen had only four concubines.
Marsha said concubines rhymes with porcupines
but Ms. Roth wouldn't tell us what they are.
Do concubines have lots of prickly quills?

We explained to the substitute, Ms. Carpenter, that
Mr. Keller had his stroke just when he was starting
to explain how to multiply and divide fractions
and that's why we only know how to use decimals.
After that, Ms. Carpenter stopped being mad at us.

In English we learned that Shakespeare may or
may not have written what Shakespeare wrote.
This disgusted everybody but most of all Todd,
who said it was as bad as Schrodinger's cat.
Ms. Roth asked him who Schrodinger was.

We learned about syllogisms. You know. Syllogisms.
All pine trees are conifers. Spruce trees are conifers too.
Therefore spruce trees are pine trees. No, wait. That
can't be right. Well then, something about this guy
named Socrates being a man and being dead.

We're studying the Constitution. America has a bicameral
legislature which means two humps. The Senate hump
has two old men from every state, even the smallest,
while the House hump is chockfull of representatives.
Oh, and the President has to be thirty-five years old.

I learned that Joe Barrish once had ringworm and
that Phil's real father died when he was only seven.
I figured out that girls are softer and tougher than boys
but just as mean and that it's calming to stare at trees
since they always know what to do and never look at us.

You Might Just Think of Me

when silence doesn't fall but
like the happy dead rises ex
nihilo to mazurka
through the Russian novel
propped against your pajamaed
knees under the maroon quilt,

when the last Trans Am pulsing
its jet black backbeat ego
dopplers down the dim divide
of your drab suburban street
humming on wet macadam
past the world's final streetlamp,

when billions of besieging
flakes bar your door, rasping
menaces against the sash
with hateful hearts, an absurd
army of bantam klansmen
silently riding the night,

then you might just think of me
stamping through wet graveyards,
a Nevsky protagonist
in a soaked greatcoat beneath
a dripping lamp, battling the
affronting snow; you just might.

To Have Seen What I Have Seen,
See What I See

It's barely autumn now, nor is
summer yet wholly out of mind.

Gray rain is falling on fallen
leaves, colder than it used to be

when that willow tree looked young,
when my wish was only to begin.

Some say that all things have their worth
and what shall be is what has been.

The raindrops dangle in a dance
on these autumnal afternoons:

summer's rain was blurred with heat,
spring's beat all, depraved and rushed;

dire will be the winter storm,
silent before the blizzard comes.

But nothing is phenomenal
about these long November rains

that show more bleakly for all their
confinement to the window panes.

These traceries I moralize
and think of weather in the mind;

yet every effort that I make
obscures the meaning that I find.

The meaning that I find feels forced,
too false to let conviction hold.

And so, it scarcely matters if
what is now is what once was

or if the window pane reflects
those pictures one already knows:

unhappiness, a child's ghost,
or joy, an old man in repose.